Poetry *in* Dangerous Times

Two Women, Two Worlds

Demetria Martínez & Susan Sherman

Casa Urraca Press

A B I Q U I Ú

Set in Bookmania and Playfair Display.

28 27 26 25   1 2 3 4 5 6 7

First edition

ISBN 978-1-956375-33-6

CASA URRACA PRESS

an imprint of Casa Urraca, Ltd.
casaurracapress.com

"These are dangerous times indeed. In such times, again and again, we turn to poets like Demetria Martínez and Susan Sherman. Here are two poets who have faced dangerous times before, always with courage, patience, compassion, and eloquence. **In the face of danger, they not only speak, but sing.** The proof is in the pages of this unique and necessary collection, two women from two different worlds showing us our common ground, the path we must walk, illuminated by the fire in these poems, to find our common humanity, to find the way home."

—Martín Espada, author of
the National Book Award-winning *Floaters*
and the Pulitzer Prize finalist *The Republic of Poetry*

"Socially engaged at all times, their work maintains a sharp yet subtle adherence to subjects that matter. The poems share an attractive economy of language, and **both poets possess a delicate elusiveness** that allows their socially concerned work to engagingly address realities in these dehumanizing times."

—Daisy Zamora, author of *The Violent Foam:
New & Selected Poems*

"What are some poets doing when they're not writing poetry? *As Poetry in Dangerous Times: Two Women, Two Worlds* reveals, **they are trying to repair the world**.... Free of didacticism and slogans, these poems address a wide range of themes and passions, always deeply moving as they remind us to struggle for social justice but also to rest and remember the people and things we love and struggle for; they are enriching and engaging."

—Irena Klepfisz, author of *Her Birth and Later Years:
New and Collected Poems 1971–2021*

"**Perhaps this is just what we need now,** now in these 'Dangerous Times': to hold onto a certain sanity found in truth-telling, if for no other reason than to inspire more truth—of histories forgotten, old-school knowledges reawakened, of movements that matter(ed), of loving that deepens wordlessly with aging. All this is found on these pages and within the years between Susan Sherman and Demetria Martínez. **Theirs is a poetics that speaks to the privilege and burden of walking one's truth.**"

—Cherríe Moraga, author of *Native Country of the Heart*

"Meet two women from two worlds: Demetria Martínez, a Chicana rooted in family history passed on, and Susan Sherman, a Jewish woman self-exiled from a family who wanted to forget. Martínez whispers poems down the page in images so tender it feels like being let in on a secret: 'Dreams opening/Like the fist of an infant.' Sherman's is a seasoned philosopher's voice simmered in 'the usual detritus of Manhattan nights' resulting in a rich stew of insights to be savored, even better the second time around. **When strong/queer/activist poets craft a gift this magnificent, take it.**"

—Mary Oishi, Albuquerque Poet Laureate Emerita and author of *Sidewalk Cruiseship*

POETRY IN DANGEROUS TIMES

This book is dedicated to those in every generation
who continue to oppose the forces
that would silence us.

Contents

83 New & Selected Poems: Susan Sherman

Two Women, Two Worlds

A Dialogue

Demetria Martínez:

I think what has shaped me most deeply as a writer is my life in New Mexico. I have always had a sense of rootedness that is symbolized in my family tree: I can trace my family's presence here going back to the 1600s, when New Mexico was part of Spain. And my Native American ancestors were present on this land even earlier, prior to both the Spanish and the American occupations. As a Chicana, I am a mestiza, a mix of European and Native ancestry.

I grew up hearing stories about Martineztown, the barrio of Albuquerque. My great-great-grandparents first settled there, hence the name. Dad loves driving through the narrow streets pointing to houses. "Your second cousin lives there, your fourth lives there." In 2023, a photographer took a picture of Dad and me standing in front of the house that was once my great-grandfather's house and store. Dad wowed the photographer with his memories of how groups of Diné used to travel by horse and buggy to buy supplies there, and how they camped out in back.

Living in New Mexico, I've prayed for peace at demonstrations outside Los Alamos National Laboratory, birthplace of the nuclear bomb. I've gone to Native dances, including to the ancient Taos Pueblo where the family watched Dad's godson dance for the first time, dust rising from beneath his moccasins. And I've made pilgrimages to the Santuario de Chimayó. Inside the nineteenth-century church is a hole replenished with earth believed to have healing powers. There, believers pray then take home little bags of earth.

All these travels and more, through swaths of desert dotted with juniper trees, beneath blue, blue skies: these wide-open spaces have shaped my work. They appear throughout my fiction: in *Mother Tongue*, a novel, and in a collection of short stories, *The Block Captain's Daughter*. My essays, *Confessions of a Berlitz Tape Chicana*, are very much rooted in my sense of place and include a piece about a visit to Trinity Site, where the first atom bomb was tested. As for my poetry? Over time my poems have become more spare, almost like haiku, reflecting the spaciousness that surrounds me. I like to think of wind blowing between each line.

Susan Sherman:

I took off for New York immediately after college, forced to leave by a difficult situation at home, and I didn't return until my mother had a stroke almost twenty years later. I sometimes describe my work as diaspora writing, not longing for a country but for family, history, a sense of belonging. I know how elusive it is to search for something you have never known, how important it is to be creative, to fashion something new. In the same spirit, I try not to manipulate my poetry, instead to let it guide me.

My biological parents were both children of Jewish immigrants from what was known as the Pale of Settlement, the large area in the Russian Empire where Jewish people were allowed to live, despite the recurring pogroms. My stepfather immigrated from Russia when he was eleven. My mother married him when I was five. None of them spoke of their roots, rarely ever spoke of their parents. They had a history they wanted to forget.

The only memory I have of my mother's parents was when I was four. Their apartment smelled like bread soaked in warm milk, in those days the food of the elderly. The one story my mother told me about my grandfather was that, in the "old country," he had married "beneath him." A revered teacher, he had fallen in love with a penniless seamstress, much to his family's horror. The irony was when they first arrived in America he couldn't get a job teaching, and she taught him to sew, and that's how they survived. I like to imagine my love of reading and learning comes from him.

Reading, particularly speculative fiction starting with the Oz books, formed the geography of my childhood. In college, my favorite classes were my philosophy courses, full of questioning and wonder. There were courses in philosophy of religion, science, psychology, politics, metaphysics. I took summer school classes so I could do a double major in philosophy and English. In New York, in the late sixties, even though I had a full-time job, I went to graduate school at night at Hunter College and got an MA in philosophy. Not because I was planning to teach, but because I loved learning so much. That deep questioning also became an integral part of my poetry, along with the magic of the image and the cadence of language.

Demetria:

My parents have always had a history they wanted to remember—and to pass down to the next generation. In 2023, folklorist Enrique Lamadrid and I did hours of interviews with Dad. I got to learn in detail about his father, Luis Sedillo Martínez. Grandpa was known throughout New Mexico for his *corridos*, or ballads. His most famous corrido, heard in jukeboxes around the state and later made into a record, was about Dennis Chávez, who was running for reelection as Senator. Like those he wrote for other candidates, the corrido praised Chávez's humble beginnings and extolled the qualities that made for a great candidate.

Then Enrique and I, with Hector Contreras, a Mexican poet, translated the corridos into English. Dad's memories, our translations, and old photos ended up as a chapbook. We gave copies to some fifty family members at a celebration in my sister's backyard—great-grandchildren among them. I swear I exhaled for the first time in months! I didn't have to worry anymore that Dad's memories would be lost to time. Later the *New Mexico Historical Review* devoted a whole issue to Grandpa. To think this project began when I found some dusty, faded broadsides of corridos in my bedroom closet. I panicked; these looked ready to crumble, so I called Enrique, who was famous for his work in literary recovery.

All my grandparents were bilingual, including Dad's mom, María Jesusita, who came to the United States in the wake of the Mexican Revolution of 1910. But, like so many of my generation, my family spoke only English at home. So I had to learn Spanish, starting in high school—and I fell in love with the language. This rich heritage is something

I celebrate in *The Block Captain's Daughter*. My character Lupe—a Mexican immigrant—is full of advice for Cory, a Chicana, who enlists Lupe in her quest to learn Spanish.

My fluency in Spanish has improved by leaps and bounds thanks to books by Latin American authors in translation—Spanish on one side, English on the other. As a writer I've been hugely influenced by "political" poets in the Spanish speaking world: Gabriella Mistral, José Martí, Rosario Castellanos, Julia de Burgos, Efraín Huerta. The list is long. Reading these poets has given me permission to take on themes such as feminism, and to write critically of our government. I don't like to fall asleep without first reading something in Spanish. The books of all these poets and more have migrated at one time or another from my bookshelves to my bed.

Susan:

Although I was born in Philadelphia, I grew up in Southern California, not the same as the Southwest, for sure, but also permeated with Spanish and Mexican culture. California, after all, was part of New Spain, and then Mexico, until the end of the Mexican American War in 1848. My first home in Los Angeles was typical faux Spanish architecture with stucco exterior paint and arched doorways. My rebellious teenage self insisted on taking French instead of learning Spanish in high school like most of my classmates. An ironic choice, given my travels to Cuba, Nicaragua, Chile, Argentina, and Mexico later in my life, when I needed to know Spanish and had to spend months studying intensively to catch up.

After I graduated from UC Berkeley in 1961, I came across country by car with two women friends—a three-week odyssey across the United States through small towns and the seemingly endless expanse of the Great Plains. The first thing that struck me on driving into the city, and I must say terrified me, was experiencing so many people and buildings crowded together. New York seemed small, cramped; especially Delancey and Suffolk, on the Lower East Side, where I had my first apartment.

The taller the buildings were, the worse the feeling of being suffocated, like those horror movies where the walls become a vice threatening to crush you. Riding on the subways was an absolute nightmare, especially during rush hour as a young woman in a short skirt, mandatory for work in those days. Instead of a hundred buildings, it seemed like a hundred hands were closing in on me, pressing against me, groping me, until I learned from observing other women how to use my elbows and my umbrella.

At Berkeley, even with over twenty thousand students in close proximity, even on the main drag where I wound up living, there was never a feeling of being crowded. If anything there was too much space. You could get lost in it. I remember the same feeling of spaciousness I had in California when I visited Albuquerque to read at the women's bookstore Full Circle for the book launch of *Naming the Waves* (Crossing Press, 1989), an anthology of lesbian poetry edited by Christian McEwen.

Demetria:

That was our first meeting. I was in my early twenties when I discovered Full Circle, which was near the University of New Mexico; it was the heyday of independent bookstores. I'd never heard of a woman-owned and woman-operated bookstore. It was there that I discovered Gloria Anzaldúa, Audre Lorde, Paula Gunn Allen, and other women writers.

After your reading I went away with issues of *IKON*, the magazine you were editing then—and I was thrilled to find poetry, essays, and articles by women of color, including lesbians.

At Full Circle and in *IKON*, I found my Chicana identity celebrated. I did not yet identify as a lesbian, and I didn't yet use the word "feminist" to describe myself. But thanks to the feminist movement of your generation, there were certain things I took for granted. I had a vague idea that I wanted to get a graduate degree and devote myself to study—and I was clear that in order to do this I could not have children. Thankfully, my parents never expressed a desire to be grandparents; I suspect that they—perhaps at a subconscious level—were influenced by feminism. Dad encouraged Mom to get her degree in early childhood education. She did and became well known for her innovative curricula.

As fate would have it, I met up with you again in Willimantic, Connecticut, a few years later when you participated in a reading sponsored by Curbstone Press. I was on the board of the press at that time. On the train ride back to New York from Connecticut, we sat opposite each other, and over the two-hour-plus trip really got a chance to talk and begin to know each other. Including that we are astrological twins—we share a birthday on the same day, July 10!

Your work was a perfect fit for Curbstone and our commitment to a literature of resistance, of witness. We published, for example, Nicaraguan poets Fr. Ernesto Cardenal and Daisy Zamora. Cardenal was Minister of Culture after the Sandinistas overthrew the Somoza dictatorship; Zamora was Vice Minister of Culture. They organized poetry workshops throughout the country to promote literacy. I went there for a poetry festival and got to read my work at a primary school. The children were in awe of poets and poetry! This was the same with everyone I met. That trip gave me a fresh vision of how poetry could penetrate the hearts and minds of ordinary folks in extraordinary ways.

Susan:

I was at the Curbstone event because in 1990 they published my book, *The Color of the Heart: Writing from Struggle and Change 1959–1990.* It was the first time I had a book published that included, along with poems, essays I had written about philosophy and about political activities I had been involved with. Activism was a major focus of my 2007 memoir *America's Child: A Woman's Journey through the Radical Sixties*, also published by Curbstone. I started the memoir with Berkeley because as children we tend to believe that the world that we grow up in, that we inhabit daily, is the only world, and it was at Berkeley I made the discovery that the world of my childhood was not the only world, that there were many alternatives, that there was the possibility of choice.

Although I scratched out some pretty dreadful poems when I was in high school, I had never read much poetry before being involved in the poetry scene at Berkeley. I remember pressing my nose up against the window of a coffee shop where a poet was reading and wishing I had the nerve to go in and take a seat myself. Finally, the end of my sophomore year, I joined the university literary magazine, *Occident*, and became friends with the editor, poet Diane Wakoski. My junior year I shared an apartment with her and her partner at the time, La Monte Young, the musician. Through them I was exposed to a whole new world of modern poetry and art centered at that time in San Francisco. It was 1959, and poetry was heavily influenced by the San Francisco Renaissance and poets like Helen Adam, Robert Duncan, Denise Levertov, John Wieners, and other poets anthologized in Donald Allen's *The New American Poetry*.

Many evenings a group of young Berkeley poets would sit in Diane's room in a circle surrounded by the light of candles stuck into empty wine bottles and read our poems. This was a whole new concept of poetry for me, where poetry was not some abstract place you visited occasionally. It was a world you lived in. After graduating, I followed my newfound love of poetry to New York which, by the early sixties, was bursting with creative energy.

Because of Diane, I was introduced to the poets at the Deux Megots coffeeshop and to Jerry Bloedow, one of the founders of the Hardware Poets Theatre, where I began to direct and write plays. We didn't have the money for a stage set for the first play I wrote and directed, *Mr. Samson, Eleanor and I*, so some friends helped me move my bedroom furniture to the loft that was our de facto theater, and I was forced to sleep on the set while the play was in production because that's where my bed was!

The poets became both friends and family. One of the closest, Ted Enslin, suggested I open up my poetic form by writing prose poems. Consequently, my poetry became more fluid and personal—despite the popular bias at the time against what was derogatively called "confessional poetry." And following a suggestion of another of the poets, Carol Bergé, I sent a poem to *El Corno Emplumado*, a bilingual literary journal published in Mexico City edited at the time by Margaret Randall and Sergio Mondragón. This initiated a correspondence with Margaret, who became one of my closest and dearest friends. In 1968, Margaret and I shared a room at the Cultural Congress in Havana.

As much as I learned during those early years to love poetry, music was my first love. I started playing the piano at the age of five, even before I started reading, and it has always influenced my writing. There was a room in the university library where you could listen to records of poets reading their work. I was captivated by the sound of their voices. Gertrude Stein, Dylan Thomas, E. E. Cummings, William Butler Yeats, Edith Sitwell, T. S. Eliot, Pablo Neruda were only a few of the many recorded. Through them, and through the contemporary poets I was beginning to live with and whose work I was beginning to know, I learned that words can also be music. They were tangible, with weight, breadth, depth. They were song.

Demetria:

I majored in Public and International Affairs at Princeton University, only to find myself also leaning toward wanting to write poetry. I took workshops with poets Ted Weiss and Maxine Kumin, a Pulitzer Prize winner. More than technique, what I learned from them was that poetry could be a vocation, a calling, as legitimate a life's work as a "real job" in investment banking, which many of my classmates planned to pursue.

After graduating in 1982, I joined Sagrada Art School, founded by a Dominican nun and painter, Sister Giotto Moots. It was based in Old Town, Albuquerque's original plaza, founded in 1706, also a home to my ancestors. I lived in an old, tiny adobe house across the street from the chapel that Sr. Giotto had built herself and that was connected to her restaurant, Joseph's Table.

Each morning, she would ring the chapel bell and students (some of whom lived in lofts that she built) would gather in the chapel to pray the Divine Office, the prayer of monks and nuns. Afterwards we enjoyed fresh bread that Giotto made each morning at Joseph's Table. I was part of this community for three years. I am forever grateful to Giotto for exhorting students to find ways to earn their living at part-time jobs so they had time to devote to their art. For a while I waited tables at the restaurant; eventually I found a part-time job as religion writer for the *Albuquerque Journal*. I also freelanced for the progressive weekly, the *National Catholic Reporter*.

My *Journal* stories ranged from the anti-Apartheid movement in South Africa to ministry to AIDS patients at the start of the epidemic. Thanks to the *Catholic Reporter* I was learning about the faith-based Sanctuary Movement: in the 1980s, Salvadoran and Guatemalans were fleeing right-wing death squads (part of dictatorships the U.S. supported in the name of fighting communism). In response, U.S. citizens defied the law by helping Central American refugees enter this country.

I knew people personally who were housing refugees, including a woman who married a man from El Salvador to keep him from being deported to almost certain death. He had been part of groups that opposed the government; influenced by "liberation theology," they worked for justice for the poor, who comprised the majority of people in El Salvador. The Sanctuary Movement began to shape my imagination as a reporter—and later as a poet and novelist.

Susan:

Activism didn't inform my writing until it became an important part of my life. A friend of mine early on said to me when I was worried about my poems, their style, their content: "You can't really change your poetry until you change yourself."

In the early sixties, I took part in the demonstrations against The House UnAmerican Activities Committee, which was still active in 1960 and held an inquiry in San Francisco. In New York, I worked with Flo Kennedy, the civil rights lawyer, and later taught at the Free School and the Alternate U, both progressive anti-establishment counter-cultural centers. I took part in anti-Vietnam war demonstrations, Angry Artists Against the War, and the Dialectics of Liberation Conference in London. I co-founded and edited *IKON* magazine in 1967, but it wasn't until my first trip to Cuba to attend the Cultural Congress of Havana in 1968 that activism became an essential part of my life and consequently my writing.

The Cultural Congress was a microcosm of progres-sives from all over the world, from Latin America and Europe and the Middle East and Africa and Asia repre-senting all the arts. As well as artists, delegates included teachers from gymnastics in grammar school to professors in college. But even more important than the papers they shared were the people themselves. It was quite different reading and talking about issues than it was interacting with people whose ideas I had previously only read about. A Vietnamese poet I struck up a friendship with gave me as a keepsake a copy of his favorite book, Walt Whitman's *Leaves of Grass*, translated into Spanish.

There was a lot of pressure not to go to Cuba during those years. I lost my job, the distribution of *IKON* was cut off when we published an issue devoted to the Cultural Congress, and I became quite ill with a duodenal ulcer from the constant stress. I returned to Cuba the following year for several months to heal, staying for a month in the hospital, living with a Cuban family in the small town of Bayamo over Christmas, and traveling around the countryside with a Cuban friend: a trip that allowed me to experience first-hand the considerable advances as well as the problems of the Cuban revolution.

In the end, the most important impact of that first trip to Cuba was how it changed me when I returned to New York. It was as if I had never really seen the city before. Previously my focus had been on what affected me. Everything else was peripheral and blurred—the poverty, the racism, the violence. I began to experience myself as inexorably linked to the world around me. It turned me from an observer of events to someone who was compelled to engage actively in the struggle for social justice, both in my personal life and, as a consequence, in my writing, which is the most intimate part of who I am.

Demetria:

In 1986, a Lutheran minister invited me to come with him to the U.S.-Mexico border. He planned to meet two Salvadoran women who had been raped by soldiers and found themselves pregnant. He was to bring them to Albuquerque as part of the faith-based Sanctuary Movement. I said yes. I'd never before witnessed someone transporting so-called illegal aliens across the border. I felt it was important to research the Sanctuary Movement in this way for a possible news story. The women were due to give birth in December, their plight evoking the story of the Biblical refugees Mary and Joseph, Jesus' parents. I ended up writing a poem about their plight, called "Nativity," and not a newspaper article—a decision that would change the course of my life.

I still can't believe what followed. In 1987, I was charged with conspiracy against the U.S. government in connection with transporting the women and inducing their entry into this country. I faced a potential twenty-five years in prison and $1.25 million in fines. The minister faced similar charges. Evidence against me included my poem. Lines from the poem still ring in my consciousness: "In my country we sing of a baby in a manger / finance death squads."

During our indictments our attorneys prepared to argue two points. First that my activities as a reporter were protected by the First Amendment. Second that the governor had declared New Mexico a sanctuary state; the minister believed that this protected his activities and, therefore, that he should be acquitted. These arguments resulted in our acquittal following a two-week trial in 1988.

I can't overstate the support we received from family, friends, and strangers leading up to our trial. Mark Rudd, a close friend who was one of the leaders of the student anti-war protests at Columbia University in 1968, spoke with poet Allen Ginsberg. A passionate supporter of freedom of speech and of the press, Allen flew to Albuquerque on his own nickel; he packed the Kimo Theater for a reading and fundraiser for our cause. I opened his reading with a poem, "Wanted," that played off of his poem "America." The first line of my poem reads: "America, our marriage is coming apart."

Our case received national and international media attention. Not the least of it came from *Ms.* magazine—thanks to a phone call Norman Mailer, whose daughter I roomed with at Princeton, made to editor Gloria Steinem. It ran after our acquittal and featured a photograph of me leaving the federal courthouse, fist in the air, triumphant—with grandma, parents, and siblings all smiles behind me.

After my trial I moved to Kansas City, Missouri, to work for the *Catholic Reporter*. In 1992, I was invited to read my poetry at a Chicano literary festival. One evening, I was seated in the back of a dark auditorium listening to Sandra Cisneros read from her short story collection, *Woman*

Hollering Creek. And suddenly, within myself, I heard the words *His nation chewed him up and spat him out.*

I felt what I can only describe as a quickening—and I felt pure joy. That night I wrote down those words on some hotel stationery. For nine months, fifty minutes a day, with a break on Saturdays, I took down what I was hearing. At times I'd say to myself: *But I have no idea how to write a novel!* What kept me going was a sense that the story was already written and afloat in the universe—and my job was to write it down.

This was how I wrote my novel, *Mother Tongue.* Set during the Sanctuary Movement, it tells the story of a Chicana and a Salvadoran refugee in love.

Susan:

My senior year at Berkeley, I sat dumbfounded as the professor lectured that contemporary creativity could only be found in literary and art criticism, while directly across the bay resounded the ongoing echoes of the San Francisco Renaissance. I never forgot that day, and a founding principle of *IKON* magazine in 1967 was the rejection of professional critics and academics mandating what was acceptable in art. We declared ourselves free of outside constraints. We set out to write about work that interested us most, whether by colleagues or strangers, and print radical political analysis alongside discussions of the tarot and alchemy. We would put the joy of discovery back into the hands of those who created it, and write about art with the same enthusiasm that went into creating it.

The Second Series of *IKON* (issues 1–14/15, 1982–1994) extended the original affirmation of the seven issues of the First Series (1967–1969). We carried over the "Creativity and Change" motto embedded in our logo, along with a slogan taken from the cover of a *Tricontinental* magazine I had brought back from Cuba: "We can and must create a new world with new forms, techniques and ideas."

Several issues in the Second Series that I am most proud of were done collaboratively: *Art Against Apartheid: Works for Freedom* (#5/6) with The Art Against Apartheid Anthology Collective; *Without Ceremony* (#9) with Asian Women United; and *The Nineties: Moving Forward, Reaching Back/A Multicultural Odyssey* (#12/13) with Coast to Coast: National Women Artists of Color.

Your and my first collaborative effort was also connected to *IKON*, resulting from participating on a panel, "Feminist Publishing Under the Gun: A Retrospective Conversation Over *IKON*'s Legacy Educating Women," at the American Educational Studies Association Conference in Seattle in 2016. The following spring, under the auspices of The Society for Educating Women, who had sponsored the panel, we co-edited a special online issue of *IKON* of original and reprinted poems, essays, and short stories by former *IKON* contributors and new contributors you added.

As an adjunct to the magazine, we opened IKONbooks in the late sixties in a building next to LaMama E.T.C. (Experimental Theatre Club), paying the rent by designing and printing their programs. We carried mostly alternative press newspapers, magazines, and books. On the weekends we sponsored musical events, political forums, and occasional benefits and quickly became an activist center.

At the time I was part of the United Committee to Combat Fascism, an activist group that did outreach for the Black Panther Party. Using our Gestetner mimeograph and electronic stencil maker, we printed a series of flyers exposing racism and promoting community control of police, which, along with their breakfast program, was a major issue the Panthers were promoting.

It is important to remember that before the internet and social media, such information was circulated almost entirely through alternative press newspapers, magazines, and books. There were few ways to be in touch, to find out what was happening in the movement both locally and nationally. We also clandestinely pasted informational posters on building walls at night with a bucket of paste and two people, one on either end of the street, as lookouts.

IKONbooks sponsored one of the first block parties in New York City and provided a space for the community at large to meet. Often children from the block used the store as a de facto play space. At one community meeting, a very belligerent man began to red bait us, shouting to our neighbors that we were a bunch of communists trying to sucker them in. Before I could say anything, a number of our neighbors stood up and not only shut up the heckler but suggested very forcefully it would be a good idea if he left. Our neighbors protected us. But even so, one night someone threw a brick through our window.

The bookstore also became a central organizing center for The Fifth Street Women's Building action, which was an attempt to combine feminism with the growing squatters movement. New Year's Eve, 1970, in the middle of a snow storm, more than two hundred women made their way into an abandoned building on Fifth Street in Manhattan to turn it into a women's center that would provide needed services for the neighborhood. Participating in this collective marked an important transition to creating the next chapter of my own "new world": feminism.

Demetria:

Through working on *IKON* with you, I came to understand and appreciate the creative work that goes into curating a magazine and physically shaping it. I've always needed some sort of creative activity to fuel my writing.

In 2016, when a painful breakup had me moving back to Albuquerque from Santa Fe, where I'd been organizing poetry workshops at a youth detention center for five years, I was at a loss what I should do with my life. Then one night I found myself at a concert where I ran into Richard Moore—one of the pioneers of the environmental justice movement—and he invited me join him and his wife, Sofia Martínez, for coffee. Early the next morning I showed up at their cozy home in the South Valley, a mostly low-income neighborhood.

First, they gave me a tour of Los Jardines Institute: a huge community garden behind the house, with row upon row of carrots, beets, tomatoes, lettuce, and much more. They explained that Jardines (Spanish for gardens), mostly run by volunteers, served people and area schools that could not otherwise afford organic produce. They took me into a studio, home to a little library of banned books, posters of Zapata and Frida Kahlo—and the site for the many cultural events Jardines sponsored.

I felt immediately at home. From then on, every Saturday I got to Richard and Sofia's early to enjoy coffee and stories about their work going back to the early years of the Chicano movement, when I was just a girl. They shared memories of setting up free health clinics in the South Valley, marching with Cesar Chavez and Dolores Huerta, and traveling to Cuba on construction brigades. I learned about Jardines' work battling polluters in the South Valley neighborhood.

Their stories, together with the caffeine, had me feeling higher than a kite. Thus inspired, Richard and I would head out to weed—or better, harvest—popping cherry tomatoes in our mouths as we picked. I can still taste the sweetness! I remain close to Richard and Sofia, though I now live about fifty minutes away, in La Cienega. I think of them as mentors and role models, as people that I want to be like "when I grow up."

During the pandemic, I came to a deeper understanding of activism. With more time to reflect and write, my poems became my form of activism. I wrote poems of witness, many focusing on border issues. Post-pandemic, with a return to our busy lives, I struggled like many to find time to write. One afternoon I was discussing this issue with my therapist, and he came up with an idea. He suggested I try writing if I wake up in the middle of the night. I answered, "That's a good idea! In only takes me an hour to write a poem because I write it ahead of time in my head and then I transcribe it." Weirdly enough, I had no memory of saying that until the next day. It was as if I'd been in a trance.

What I told him does in many ways ring true. I'm not the type who can write for hours at a time. What happens is that I "hear" a line of poetry and I write it down. Then I go clean the kitchen—and my subconscious takes over and I "hear" more words. Then the next day or week I write down those words until a poem is birthed.

Susan:

Being isolated and teaching online during Covid gave me a chance to reflect on my forty-three years at Parsons School of Design. I admit to sometimes cursing teaching for taking time and energy from my writing. It wasn't until my retirement two years ago that I began to realize how important my experience teaching was for me, both as a writer and as an activist. I had to communicate complex ideas to undergraduates in a way that they could relate to them, and this had a profound effect on my poetry. How to say things directly without losing depth or meaning.

I lost my first teaching job at Mannes College of Music when I returned from the Cuban Cultural Congress in 1969 and didn't teach again until I was hired part-time in 1979 in the Foundation Year Philosophy Department at Parsons. In the intervening years I had taken whatever jobs I could get, from waitressing to computer typesetting. From my first year at Parsons I participated in the struggle to unionize part-time teachers. Our initial attempt failed because the school lawyers found legal technicalities and invalidated the election. We finally won our first union contract on our second attempt in 2004, when we joined UAW Local 7902.

During my time teaching, I moved from first-year foundation philosophy to a variety of electives ranging from analyzing the pros and cons of technology to tracing the cultural history of media, examining the history of language, and exploring visual culture in the context of the radical sixties, my last elective course before I retired. I also taught a first-year writing seminar that coordinated with a creative art course for eight years, two of them online during Covid. All of this rich material added to my own work.

In *IKON* 12/13, we reprinted bell hooks' essay, "an aesthetic of blackness: strange and oppositional," which advocates an aesthetic that brings together art and revolutionary politics in a way that enlarges rather than limits the parameters of the artist's vision. It is a beautifully written work that I featured in many of my classes and has served through the years as a guide and personal inspiration.

But perhaps most important was learning not to dictate what students should or should not believe—encouraging critical thinking, steering them away from rhetoric and the blind acceptance of established conclusions, so they could learn to make their own way through images of the world around them, which are often violent and make no sense. Little did I realize when I first began teaching that it would turn into a lifelong vocation and once again take me in a direction I had never anticipated.

Demetria:

Another huge turning point in my own life—right up there with my trial—was my diagnosis, at age thirty, of bipolar disorder. My then-husband and I were in Nevada on what was supposed to be a vacation. We were at a diner. I remember gazing out the glass window: it was dark and we were surrounded by desert. I hadn't slept for three nights. For three nights I had walked the halls of our motel; I understood in my gut why forced insomnia was a tool of torture. I felt like I was going mad.

By some miracle I remembered the phone number of a family friend, a doctor. I left the diner and walked out to a phone booth, called collect. I asked him if he could ship overnight a few sleeping pills to hold me over till we got back to Albuquerque. He started asking me questions.

Do your moods tend to go up and down, Demetria? Highs and lows? I paused for a long time and wondered. About the sadness that would strike out of nowhere, a sadness so dark I couldn't get out of bed in the morning. And highs? I thought of all the times I would sit at a picnic table in a nearby park, breathlessly beholding the beauty of a rock, convinced I should join a convent so I could spend my life contemplating creation: a high that rapidly descended into irritability, anger, insomnia and self-loathing.

He asked me other questions then said, *I think you might have something called bipolar disorder.* He said he would make an appointment for me with a specialist he knew. I just remember smiling. It was as if he'd held a mirror up to me. I saw myself but in a new light. I was not to blame for all the times I was unable to function like a normal human being. It was not a failure of character; the problem was brain chemistry that could be treated.

For a long time I was afraid of writing about my bipolar disorder. I felt ashamed, fearful that others would think of me as "crazy." And indeed, a fine line runs between me and the guy on the street muttering to ghosts. I've had the privilege of excellent health care, which has included a stay in a hospital for mania. I've come to see that with such privilege comes a responsibility: to write compassionately about my journey, and to celebrate the humanity of all who struggle with mental health issues.

Now when I think of bipolar disorder I think of it as a journey—a journey that has given rise to a number of poems. Fortunately, I never romanticized my condition. I never believed for a moment that untreated mental illness makes for better writing. On the contrary, I have worked closely with my doctors—and have achieved what I can only describe as remission. I write now out of a place of stability. This stability, or centeredness, has brought with it tremendous gifts, not least among them marriage to an amazing woman. I am learning not to fear feelings that are simply part of the human condition, such as grief or sadness.

And the highs? I love nothing more than feeding our goats and hens then sipping tea on a swing beneath our apricot tree. And I love nothing more than praying the rosary each morning, a practice that, paradoxically, gives me a "high" and at the same time grounds me. I figure if the rosary, and Mass, were good enough for my grandma—and all my grandmas before her—they're good enough for me. And that has proven true.

Susan:

Jewish was a name given me before I was born, before my own name Susan was given me. Jewish was a place I was born into. For me, in 1939, in Philadelphia, it was a safe place. For my parents, my grandparents, immigrants, the children of immigrants, it was a place of alternating terror and pride.

One of the most powerful and damaging things my parents taught me, by their words and by their actions, was the necessity to hone the ability to hide. They were haunted during the years of my childhood by their own history, by World War II and the Holocaust, by the widespread anti-Semitism in their adopted country.

People spoke their prejudice openly in front of my mother with her blond hair and blue eyes, not knowing she was Jewish, and she would bring their words home to us as a lesson. "Be wary of anyone who isn't Jewish. No matter how close you think you are, one day they will call you a dirty Jew." At the time, it never occurred to me how many of my parents' choices and their attitudes were driven by insecurity and fear. And how deeply they affected me.

For me, in 1959, what it meant to be a lesbian a decade before the movement was what was most problematic, when I knew of no one to turn to for advice or comfort, no community, no literature, and two therapists who told me it was a pathology, a developmental aberration.

How hard it was for me to express openly how I felt as others coming out in the midst of the lesbian/feminist movement in the late sixties and the early seventies wrote about their experience with ease. How hard it was to make them understand why it was so difficult for me to say the word *lesbian* aloud even though I had been saying it in poems indirectly for years, from the first love poem I wrote in 1961.

And now, the pendulum has swung again because of the conflation of being Jewish with the unconscionable reaction of Isreal to the horror of October 7, 2023, its reign of death on the Palestinian people enabled by our American bombs and munitions, and its continuing refusal to end the occupation of Palestinian territory.

Silence. From perceived necessity, from shame. Not wanting to reveal myself, to stand out, to feel it is dangerous to do so. Wanting to pass as normal, to fit in. First I used words to shield me, and then finally to open me to who I am.

Demetria:

You grew up during World War II, and I remember, as a ten-year old, seeing images of the Vietnam War on TV and in Dad's *Time* magazines: the little girl running down the street, screaming with pain from napalm, and the Buddhist monk who set himself on fire to protest the war. Dad was in the Marines and I recall the terror I felt that he might be called to fight. I began reciting Hail Marys in my bed each night, praying for the war to end.

It was only in the late 1990s that I came to grips with Vietnam, thanks to an invitation to teach at the summer writing workshops at the William Joiner Center for the Study of War and Social Consequences at the University of Massachusetts, Boston. The center brought together American and Vietnamese veterans of the war who were also poets and writers. These included novelists Tim O'Brien and Larry Heineman and poets George Evans and Kevin Bowen. Also on the faculty were authors whose lives had been touched by war: I became close to Salvadoran poet Claribel Alegría and Nicaraguan poet Daisy Zamora. Activist writers also participated, including Grace Paley and Martín Espada.

My most precious memories are of rooming with Lady (Adelaide) Borton. I co-taught a memoir class with her. A humanitarian worker during and after the war, she learned Vietnamese. Her extensive writings include translations of Vietnamese women poets. She taught me something I have never forgotten: she explained she never used the phrase "Vietnam War" because for the Vietnamese it was the American War. The Americans were the ones who dropped the bombs.

As we're talking, Trump has just won the presidential election for the second time. I know I can't give in to despair. I know I have to turn my energy into continuing to help build communities of resistance. We have to care for each other so we will have the inner resources to move forward. Above all, we also need to be very creative about where we go from here and to learn from the experiences of people who've been in struggle for generations.

Susan:

It has been more than six decades since I made that choice at Berkeley to take an alternative route from the one my family had proscribed for me, literally a leap into the unknown. I had no idea what would happen when I left for New York, I had no idea of the consequences when I went to Cuba, when I started *IKON* magazine, when I went to Nicaragua or Chile, when I started teaching, when I had my first relationship with a woman.

We both grew up against a background of war. One of my earliest memories was my family clustered around our huge console radio that dominated the room, transfixed by President Truman announcing the United States had dropped an atomic bomb on the Japanese city of Hiroshima. It was August 6, 1945. I was six years old.

During my second trip to Cuba in the fall of 1969, I was invited to a meeting with a Vietnamese delegation and some dozen American students. The Vietnamese praised us for choosing to stand against the war; they had no choice, had to fight. I was shocked at their incredible generosity. Their approach made me even stronger in my resolve to fight not only against the Vietnam War, but all unjust wars as well.

When many are so polarized, when more and more we seem to be insulating ourselves within our separate enclaves, when our names often carry an extensive list of identifying adjectives attached to them, when stereotypes run rampant, our collaboration, this dialogue between us, seems to me to be even more important now than ever.

New & Selected Poems
Demetria Martínez

Inauguration Day

A Mexican nun once
Told me: to refry beans
Add a touch of milk
If you don't have lard.
Remember that, friends
Write it down, write down
All such tips from foremothers
Who lived through such times
Who knew to add extra
Onion for flavor, still more
Onion to stretch the meal.
We have so many to feed
And ourselves to nourish
Gathering strength to pull
The curtain behind which
The conqueror cowers.
Hot tortillas, splendid table
We hold hands, say
The blessing: pass
The pepper, pass
The salt.

Birthday

I was born in the Year of the Rat
Black lung from the smoke
Of burning American flags
First poems penned by
The rocket's red glare
Math was simpler
Fifty-eight thousand soldiers
And then there were none
I was born in the Year of the Rat
Thirty-eight years a life
Still at half-staff.

Borders

Someday borders will be no more
Because too many people died crossing
Because still more people survived
Walls will come tumbling down
Monarch butterflies and children
Will dance among the ruins
Fields of sunflowers will spring
Up over the graves of the fallen
Their names—María, José, Jesús—will be inscribed
In a new poetry that will not let us forget.

Marriage, for Camilla

A breeze sweetens
Our fingers as we walk
Among the lilacs
In the shade
Of the apricot tree
That sprung
From a pit your dad
Spit out on the dirt
Decades ago
When you see that two
Women can't work
Together, he said, *call Abe*
But you did it
With a friend
Built a house of adobe
Like the mud nest
Swallows built
This spring
In the corner
Of the porch
Two swallows
Two women
Gathering apricots
To freeze
For the winter
And beyond.

Rear Views

For Rachel Dolores

She used to drive
Me crazy, my mother
In the rearview mirror
Donning her Avon lipstick
Before easing out of the driveway
I was five years old
I was in a rush
To arrive
Ernie Pyle Library
The children's room
Where books smelled like
A forest after a storm
I sat on the floor
Enlightenment came easy
If not, there was always
The card catalog, tarot
Of titles.

I'm older now, in no
Rush to arrive
I, too, feel naked
Without my lipstick
Without a book to open
Like a Japanese screen
Behind which I rest, dream
And rise, then read
Some more until
You arrive.

War

Dad covers his retablo of St. Francis
With the Ukrainian flag
A dove resting in the saint's hand
Hidden now in blue and yellow silk
Dad says he wishes he could go help
He's a Lieutenant Colonel
In the Marine Corps Reserves
A specialist in secret codes
Only he's eighty-six, retired now
And every night has to help mom
Walk from her recliner
To her chair at the kitchen table
It's mid-April, still no rain
Some days all you can do is watch
A flag whip in the March winds.

So Much Depends

On an accent mark
Our name was Martín
Until great-grandpa Trinidad
Changed it to Martínez
So that no one
Would call us Martin
I may be the only cousin left
Who strikes the *i* with a lightning bolt
I stand in that light
And am seen.

La Promesa

For Sonia (born and died May 26, 2001)

You floated with the majesty
Of a storm
Into life
And into death

We made a home
For you but you carried off
The roof
We cupped our hands
But your sweet
Waters turned to ash

You wreaked so much
Hope and havoc, hacking away
At our dead roots
We are wanderers again
In clay and ink, remaking
Our covenant to become
The eye of the storm
El ojo de dios

There is no promised land
But the promise is good
You said you would
Come and you did
Huracán, rainbow
Palo verde twig
In the beak of a hummingbird.

Mother

Because she will never again
Plant roses in the backyard
Because she will never again
Set out raisins for robins
What remains of her life
Cuts through me like a river

I hear the ripple of her breath
It's still too early
The monarchs have not yet arrived
She calls my name
Then can't remember why

I wait with her in the blue room
Witness to what remains of her life
Food, drink and sleep
Silence vast as the sky

Mommy, mama, mom
Because she will never again
Hear my cry, or see the stars
That scar the night.

Hope

For Mark Rudd
In memoriam, Paul Rudd

Sometimes the pain
Is so great that the word
Hope
Must be buried
In the dust

So for now
I offer these words
From my land
Cottonwood
Parsley, fig
Dandelion
Pink cosmos
I offer the
Howl
Of coyotes
The aroma
Of a bonfire
And a blue
Egg from the
Chicken coop

Sometimes the pain
Is so great
That the word
Hope
Must be
Buried
In the dust.

Winter Solstice

For Israel and Palestine,
December 1, 2023

Wild white world
Calligraphy of crows
Bare branches bend
Wind song whistling
The Ortiz Mountains
Wrapped in a
White shawl as
Fat flakes fall
Still and silent
As a truce
As a prayer
May it hold
Even in this brutal cold.

Wanted

After Allen Ginsberg, 1988

America our marriage is coming apart
I've done everything right, got my degree
Now you tell me my English won't do
America I'm not good enough for you?
Better my Spanglish than your smooth talk America
No, I won't sleep with you, not now not ever
Ah come on America, all I wanted was a little
Adobe house in Atrisco, a porch swing
Two niños, some democracy
Now I read in the *Albuquerque Journal*
That you left me for a younger woman
Bought guns for drugs, drugs for guns
Destroyed Managua in order to save it
Spied on Communist Maryknoll nuns in Cleveland
America your face is on wanted posters
In post offices and I'm on sleeping pills again America
Last night I dreamed the Pentagon was a great
Ouija board spelling out REPENT REPENT
In half sleep I reached for you love but got
Only a scent of amber waves of grain
I got up for a hit of caffeine, the Book of Psalms
And whoosh, I saw the promised land
You don't need citizenship papers there
It's colored and smells of refried beans

Remember, remember who you are America
Purple mountain majesty above fruited plains
Worked by mexicanos, America call off your dogs
America give me a green card though I don't qualify
America forgive me if I gag your memory
At La Paloma Bar on South Broadway
America I'm twenty-seven and tired thanks to you
And thanks to you I found God on a stoop on Arno Street
America you claim crime's fierce in this neighborhood
I tell you it's nothing next to your crimes
The wars we fund start at the package liquor store
And end twice a year at confession
America I don't want progress, I want redemption
Cut the shit, we could be lovers again, don't hang up
America I'm your dark side, embrace me and be saved
Pull yourself up by your bootstraps, I know you can
America I'm not all bitter, I'm a registered Republican
At parties when friends ask, *America who?*
I introduce you, explain you've
Had a difficult upbringing
But I can't cover up for you America
Get that straight, honey it's not
Too late, it's not too late
America the ball's in your court now.

Blessing Poem at the Emergency Room

Bless the paramedic, Cristina
Who placed her hand
On my shoulder
And whispered
It's OK, breathe

Bless the nurse
Whose name I forget
Who broke the rules
And charged my phone
So that I could tell
My sister that I am
Among the living

Bless Dr. Sodenberg
Emergency room doctor
Who had me adjust
My mask then gave me
A hug

Bless the little boy
Who lost a layer
Of skin on his left hand
At a baseball game
I promised his mother
I would pray for him
She smiled

It was all I could do
Sometimes
It is all I can do.

Tears

Drenched my face
When you said
You were moving away
To a town
Called Dolores
The Spanish word
For sorrow

And what of French
Italian, Portuguese?
Will I spend the rest
Of my life translating
My grief?

We Meet in Your Backyard

In the shade of a cottonwood
I speak of my pain
Of a body I do not care for
Hair growing gray, sagging breasts
Then a butterfly with black and yellow
Wings lands inside the mouth of a tiger lily
While you aim your camera, take a picture
I draw a deep breath
Forget my pain.

The Dress Daisy* Gave Me

1.
Flaming sunflowers
Fire of red and gold mouths
Mouths and tongues
The end of Somoza began
As whispers against Somoza
A plan, a plan and a song
Notes ascending until the lie shattered
Turning wine into water
Water into crops.

2.
She tells me
The most unlikely soils
Give way to love
Stems and seeds
And that the most unlikely love
Begins as a dream
Of rice and oil and the shriek
Of onions
The setting out of plates
A spray of green elephants
On Indian cotton
Hanging in the doorway
To another room.

3.
I feel the flaming mouths
Against my bare skin
I wear this for you
Though you cannot see me
It might be years
Before our fingers curl together
In my heat like these leaves
Years.

4.
The sunflower dress
Hangs on a hook
As I take the receiver
From its cradle
The end of our solitude
Began in whispers
Dreams cracking open like shells
Seeds, salt on our lips
Dreams opening
Like the fist of an infant.

*Nicaraguan poet Daisy Zamora was a combatant of the
Sandinista Liberation Front, which overthrew the Somoza
dictatorship, and served as Vice Minister of Culture after the
1979 revolution.

Clock

For George Evans

Wear a watch
That does not work
Because minutes lie
Because hours are nails
In the heart of God
Let the hands of time
Tame you instead
Fingers of shadow
Fingers of light
The sun sets sail
The sun docks
Time is scrawled
On the sidewalk
Open the curtain
Look in on your life
Against the laughter
Of eternity
Are you reading?
Are you weeping?
Are you setting out
A blue bowl of fruit?

Holiness flowers in
The fissures of this day
Steep the seconds
Like manzanilla
Wrap yourself
In the steam
Of centuries
Take time's pulse
Hot in your own hands.

The Peach Tree

I wanted to pick
A peach to press
Into your palm
Picture-perfect
Ready for your lips
But all I found
Was one that
Fell on the ground
Pecked at by birds
Will you take it?
Just like me?
Sweet but bruised?
Bruised but sweet?

For Dr. Dunklee

Yes, I know
Of other
Trees
But I have
Come
To trust
Your shade
Especially
The way
Even when my winds
Blow strong
Your leaves
Never fall.

On a Table

In the waiting room
Vogue magazine
On the cover a
Model refuses
To smile at me.

Despite decades
Of face creams
Sunscreens
Crow's feet
Ring my eyes
Brown flecks
Spot my cheeks
Despite decades
Of advertisements
I am not young
I am not white.

Remember María

Remember how she walked
Across the waters
Of the Rio Grande
Remember how she flashed
Her passport
With a photo
Of our Lady of Guadalupe
At the border guards
Remember how she waved
A broom like a wand
At work wielded rags
And buckets until
Your house shone
There are thousands
Of Marías with dark
Eyes that watch you
Don't turn away
Or you'll miss
A miracle
A story
Of a nation
Being born
Beneath
The North Star.

You Built a House

For my grief
You built a house
For my joy
Then gave me
A mirror
Of beveled glass
The hammer
Was heavy
The nail
Sharp
But I hung
That mirror
By myself
And could
At last see
That all along
The builder
Was me.

Consuelo

Now Connie
Like having
Her hair cut
Too short
Easier to
Pronounce
Her kindergarten
Teacher said.

It will take years
For Connie
To grow
Her name back
To look
In the mirror
And love
What she sees.

Rose Lipstick

What I took
From mom's drawer
To wear
To her funeral
Now forever
In my purse
Those years
Of *Glamour*
Magazine
Seventeen
Magazine
Sampling
Lipsticks
At the
Department
Store
But the secret
Was there
All along
On mom's
Lips
When she smiled
At us kids
A rose
In full bloom.

If Things Had Been Different

We could have been lovers
Your arms encircling me
But they'd already taken
My mug shot, in a windowless
Cell with no name
Fingerprints too
Blue ink pad
Never to be erased
We would have been lovers
But it was too late
I was a woman
In a cell
Stained.

Yesterday God Was Everywhere

In the okra you planted
The squash, beets, chives
Cosmos, morning glories
You dug into the earth
With your fingers
That earlier in the day
Traced my furrows, my lips
We waited a long time to plant
But then it rained all night
Wet kisses on the breath of the earth.

Grandmother

The cottonwood tree on fire
Gold and red leaves
Color the swing
Where I sit
In one hand, tea
In another, rosary beads
Sixty-three years
How I wish to become
My grandmother
Nothing a Hail Mary
Couldn't heal
Or manzanilla tea
The way autumn opened
Its wings to her
Bead by bead.

If I Knock

Will you open
The door?
Will you know me
Though I'm wearing
A mask?
Will you reach
For me through
The flames?
Can we still
Call this love
Our eyes
Burning
On this scrap
Of a planet
A firestorm
That cannot
Be put out?

Mania

Instead of choosing
To be the singer, I chose to be
The song
Instead of choosing
To be the giver of light, I chose
To be the light
Too beautiful
Too bright
I paid the price.

Activities Director

She gave me *Moby-Dick* (Large Print) and
The History of Art (Marilyn on the cover)
Still, there were bars on the windows
On the other side of the impossibly tall fence
Crows pecked at the asphalt, hungry
Like me, for what I don't know
At least the crows could fly
At least the wind carried them home
While I could only bend the bars
In my dreams.

Christmas

Love too vast to squeeze into haiku
Not vast enough to span the miles
Postage stamps will have to do
Touch my signature while the ink is still wet

Where to next? China? Venezuela?
Yet you say you want bread baked in an horno
Give me your forwarding address
Break open the round loaf while it's still hot

Carolers knocked on your door last night
Who was the woman who passed out cups of apple cider?
You said you wanted to hear "Silent Night" in Spanish
She offers comfort and joy in English

Should you visit me you will not get lost
Luminarias light the way to my house
I will keep my door unlocked through the night
Come while the candles still burn bright.

For English Press One (A True Story)

You have reached _____
If this is a medical emergency
Please hang up and dial 911
To continue this call in English please
Press one, para Español, oprime el nueve
Please listen carefully as our menu options
Have recently changed
If you need to cancel or schedule
An appointment press one now
If you are sick and need to speak
With a nurse press three
We're sorry, we did not understand that
If you need to cancel or schedule
An appointment press one
If you are sick and need to speak
With a nurse press three
We're sorry, we did not understand that
For billing press two
We're sorry, all of our representatives
Are currently busy or helping other customers
If you know the extension of the party
You are trying to reach, please press one now
Otherwise, press two

You have reached billing
Due to the high volume of calls
We are experiencing, we ask that you
Leave your number after the tone
And one of our representatives
Will return your call shortly
If you have reached this number in error
Press one to return to the main menu
We're sorry, you have reached a number
That has been disconnected
Please hang up and dial again.

May 13, 2022

Flames eat house after house
Weeds tumble across roads
As cars snake south from Española
What would I pack if it were me?
Grandpa's poems? Grandma's doilies?
Or, terrified, would I up and flee
With every memory I could fit
Into a red truck with three dogs
And the woman I love?

Haiku*

For Camilla, again

My boat rocks
On the wave
Of your smile

*This haiku came to me in a dream. When I woke up,
I wrote it down.

Advent

We are waiting
For the birth
Of the child
Who speaks
In tongues
Arabic, Hebrew
Who, with
Lifted hand
Deflects a bullet
A baby
Who smells
Of roses
A baby
Pulled from
The rubble
Eyes shimmering
Like stars.

Dreamers* Talk Back to the Border Patrol

Because you cannot detain clouds
And clamoring rain
Because you cannot detain
A blizzard of apple blossoms
Because you cannot detain the scent
Of honeysuckle and blue corn soup
Love, too, evades your searchlight
Love flits like a butterfly from sky to sky
Because you cannot detain a dream
We are your worst nightmares

*Dreamers refers to undocumented immigrants who were brought to the United States as children.

Ars Poetica (at age 61)

Hurry, gather what you can
The mountains are scarved in smoke
Bloodied with flames
You don't have the time you once did
And a sorrow no pill can heal
Draws tears that would restore
The earth if they could fall
From the sky
Hurry, gather what you can
In your green spiral notebook.

You Tell Me There Is a Place

In the universe for those
Who wrestle with demons
Tell me: what did the devil
Do with my lost years?
Did he eat them?
Did he fall into a sound sleep
And so spare a single soul from pain?
I don't think so
And why, all these years later
Must I forgive him long enough
To touch with love
All that was lost?
Forgive myself long enough
To write these poems?

What to Do If You Can't Afford a Doctor

Above all, think positive thoughts
They say it will add years to your life
Above all, laugh a lot
A study showed it might help cure your cancer
Above all, practice meditation
It's free, and all you need do
Is observe your pain in a detached fashion
Above all, visualize: picture good little white cells
Gobbling up bad little brown cells
Above all, take vitamins and minerals
Herbal tea and leafy greens
Avoid caffeine, dairy, gluten
Try Downward Facing Dog
Above all, make lists
Make a list of your goals
Make a list of things
You're grateful for
Make a list of things
You need to make lists of
Above all, remember
Early to bed, early to rise
God helps those who help themselves
What goes around comes around
Above all don't stress

Draw a smiley and tape it to the refrigerator
Write BREATHE and tape it to the bathroom mirror
Write THINK POSITIVE THOUGHTS
And tape it to the front door
So, you can't afford a doctor?
Just be sure to put your affairs in order
And don't worry about a thing.

Death

Yes, it helps that I believe
In heaven
And yes, it helps that heaven
Turns out to be
Around the corner from a stand
Of snow-laden cottonwoods
Outside an old adobe church
Iglesia San José, where even
The youngsters sing
The Our Father in Spanish
And the old folks in metal chairs
Finger wooden rosary beads
And yes, it helps
That heaven turns out to be
Among the toppled
Tombstones in the church yard
Stones adorned with pink
Plastic flowers
That one day someone
Will place
By my faded name.

Like God the Rooster Crows

At all the wrong times
Trying to wake me up
Some days I hear
Some days I don't
When I don't the darkness hovers
And I am searching, seeking
To become one with the light once again.

Nativity: For Two Salvadoran Women, 1986–1987

Your eyes, large as Canada, welcome
this stranger.
We meet in a Juárez train station
where you sat hours,
your offspring blooming in you
like cactus fruit,
dresses stained where breasts leak,
panties in purses tagged
Hecho en El Salvador.
Your belts, like equators,
mark north from south,
borders I cannot cross
for I am a North American reporter,
pen and notebook, the tools
of my tribe, distance us
though in any other era I might
press a stethoscope to your wombs,
hear the symphony of the unborn,
finger forth infants to light,
wipe afterbirth, cut cords.

You tell me, *It is impossible*
to raise a child in that country.
Sister, I am no saint.
Just a woman who happens
to be a reporter,
a reporter who happens
to be a woman,
squat in a forest, peeing
on pine needles, watching you
vomit morning sickness,
a sickness infinite
as the war in El Salvador,
a sickness my pen and notebook
will not ease.
Tell me, ¿Por qué están aquí?
How did you cross over?
In my country we sing
of a baby in a manger,
finance death squads,
how to write of this shame,

of the children you chose to save?
It is impossible to raise a child
in that country.
A North American reporter,
I smile, you tell me you are due
in December, we nod,
knowing what women know.
I shut my notebook,
watch your car rock
through the Gila Wilderness.
A canoe hangs over the windshield
like the beak of an eagle
as babies turn in your wombs,
summoned to Belén to be born.

At Last

Love, say it
Love, play it
Like scales
The major
And the minor
Of it
You will try
To trap it
You cannot
Trap it
So, you
Reintroduce it
Like a wolf
Into the wilderness
And dream, dream
For centuries
To come
Until the word
Can be heard
Above the cry
And the gun.

New & Selected Poems

Susan Sherman

There Was a Woman Once

who was more to me than words
any blending of alphabet   and sound
We met at the corners of day
in the space where night crosses light
where shadows fold into darkness
The moments between our meetings
were air   Fifty years lie between her
and this poem   a length of time
impossible to render

There was a woman once who was more
to me than imagination   wonder
the chimeras that embrace the night
More than the chill kiss of wind that tortured
her secret into patterns of light and
breeze   A woman who was more to me than
forever   the bending of syllable and time

We met on a hilltop in Vermont   made love
in the sweetgrass of our desire
These are moments that defy forgetting
These are moments time cannot cure with
detail noise distraction   Mornings that bound us
sticky and tight   with dew

There was a woman once who was more to
me than flesh   We touched to open
and then once again to close
the way a negative is held over wary eyes
to keep the sun from blinding in the madness
of its fire   What lay between us was that
strong   What joined us was that fierce
Lying in each other's arms

Married   she had never meant for us to happen
had seen me as diversion   a momentary lapse
Now she called me treasure   promised
to keep me always   cherished
hidden   in her private place
but forever is a length of time like any other

One afternoon   precisely at the stroke of one
she lapsed into a silence without boundary
The air lay like a tomb around us
She could not look at me   touch me   say my name
She had never meant it to go so far
It had become too much for her to bear
This woman who meant more to me
than words

Should I be grateful   thank whatever gods
or goddesses   gifted me this passion   this legacy
I cannot relinquish   cast aside
Forever is a length of time without forgiveness
After all these years   I search for her no longer
but for that moment between opening and
distance   when I held her close
Not yet knowing enough to turn away

Border Guards

There are lines drawn in the sand
that must never be crossed   So say the pundits
the arbiters of boundaries definitions   of what should
or should not be said   or done   There are lines
drawn on maps   around cities boroughs neighborhoods
blocks houses   The people who live in them

There are lines drawn around nations
Lines teeming with people waiting to get in
or out   There are lines drawn around individuals
ethnic racial tribal lines   Around genders   he she they
you me them   A demarcation of countries
cultures continents

There are lines drawn around hemispheres
North South East West   Around the Earth itself
There are longitude lines latitude lines
The Tropic of Capricorn is a line The Tropic of Cancer
The earth as it circles space As we delineate the seasons

A child takes a crayon   weighs it carefully in her palms
It is yellow   the color of the sun   or of her dreams
places she sees in the pictures she thumbs through at night
her fingers scrolling color across paper   purple
then blue   an ocean   then fire blazing orange
subtle green trees flowers objects without set form
Only she knows what they mean

Lines of memory are like that   vivid weightless
ghost images without boundary   Cézanne
seeing a forest of trees come into being
in the dawning sun   paints them obsessively
branches leaves undulating out of birthing light
as they come alive in front of his discerning eyes

All this is not to say we do not need to name things
identify them ourselves   but where exactly are these
boundaries borders guarded so carefully
with passports rules and laws These lines that
label us define us   separate us   These lines
that must never be crossed

What We See

World War II   1940s USA   Paranoia permeates
every corner of our Jewish home   The visual indicator
of beauty approval acceptance   the ability or inability
to hide   the length and structure of the nose

Born to blackouts every evening   songs of soldiers
marching from a nearby base at early dawn
I was blessed with a small ski-jump astride my face
My sister not so lucky   at eighteen welcomed
a beautiful new appendage from which to breathe

My stepfather   behind his back   nicknamed "runt"
A cruel caricature   twin brother to the fabled witch
Thick body   crooked nose   as if pieces of him
had forgotten how to grow

Eleven years old   an immigrant   fighting
his way up from poverty to a measure of success
he acquired my mother   blue-eyed blonde petite
as trophy wife

She could pass where he could not   be accepted in places
that shut him out   Appearance denying him an entrée
even his newly won riches could not buy

Equal parts caring and abusive   racist to the core
he saw himself reflected   looked down upon   despised
like hated others   They deserved nothing   and neither
in his mirrored self did he

My mother   oblivious to anything outside
her silhouetted frame   had left her own impoverished
past behind   turned her back on immigrant parents
Never again to speak their names

Growing into the 1960s   denying my own parents in turn
Their values   expectations   their past no longer
a conscious part of mine   I recognized
a more dominant oppression   color
A racism endemic to our adopted home

Anger crowding every corner of my mind
in spite of all my poetry soul-searching activism rage
I was also deluded by surface symbols
visual stereotypes of others   and myself

Jewish   Lesbian   Privileged in more ways than one
True daughter of a mother who didn't look the part
I imagined I could hide   choose when and if and what
I decided to let others see

2019   almost a century has passed   The merciless struggle
to listen   to let others in   to look beneath the surface remains
To recognize discrete individuals behind coined clichés
To fight the stereotypes that foster hate   The invisible nose
of childhood still firmly plastered on my face

First and Last Poems

For Violeta Parra

there is nothing romantic
about death   about pain
tears falling like soft clouds
like copper clouds   the color of rusted blood
the texture of fire

the first enemy is fear
the second   power
the third   old age

all my life   all those books   all those feelings
words   thoughts   experiences
to say such simple words   to feel
such simple things

your mountains   like my own   like home
rows of dust   of light brown soil
as if a gentle wind could level them
could blow them away

the sea   touching my nostrils
filling them   a country of smell
of sound   of wine   flowers   of salt air
of early morning   opening and
opening through my mind
my heart   the extremities
of my hands my feet

if I were a bird and could float
dipping and weaving tapestries of air
and light   if we could fly together
like silver crows   birds of dream
until everything stops   is silent and
gentle   like your songs   your voice

but the world allows us nothing
the world is nerves   is fiber
dust and sand   the world changes constantly
nothing remains the same

I see you singing into the air
as if your voice could fly   be free
were there creatures above you
listening   fishing your gifts
from the breeze   was there a place
that could hold you as you opened yourself
to it   as you went where no one else
could follow   where no one else
could see

> *each time I have loved*
> *I have left part of myself behind*
> *until now I am mostly memory*
> *mostly dream   what I have left*
> *I give to you   my last love*
> *my last song*

> *the total of all*
> *I have ever felt or known*

we grow smaller as we grow
as things empty themselves of us
and we   of them

it is so deep   this thing between us
no name can contain it
even time trembles
at its touch

Imagine a Globe Spinning Through Space

You are standing in Canada   The stars are
singularly bright   You watch them in silence
You are standing in China   Bikers struggle
through crowded streets   Pollution so dense
it obscures the light   You are standing in Spain
It is summer   The sun burns your flesh
as you reach toward your daughter's hand
You are standing in Africa   The Serengeti is quiet
Predators wait for night   You are standing in Antarctica
the sky dimming in preparation for winter's long sleep
You are standing at the North Pole   or in a big city
Calcutta perhaps   or Moscow Buenos Aires New York
You are standing in the suburbs   on the plains
on an island   Do you ever think it curious
no matter where you are   freed of gravity
you will fall into space   Perhaps even now you
slant at a ninety degree angle   or worse
with your head hanging permanently down
How athletic to be stretched out sideways
rigid as a board   What determination to remain
the wrong way round   the soles of your feet where
your head should be   Have you ever considered
how distorted our perception of who we are
how we are placed might be   when we are   all of us
standing every which way   but up

Requiem

Think of the lowly mouse   No one to mourn her
shed a tear   Gray   ugly   tiny ears laid flat
a smaller version of a rat

No country mouse   Disney cartoon with gleaming
patent leather fur   round megaphone ears
she is a city dweller   infested with germs

wanting only a warm place to nest
a drink of water   a meal   Think of her
the common mouse   murdered in an act

of self-defense   dumped unceremoniously into garbage
covered by banana peels   toilet paper   bottle caps
days-old food   Perhaps she is a mother

her children waiting patiently for her return
Think kindly of her   the common mouse
who had no say over who she was   where she was born

her position in life   No obituaries
will honor her   No interviews   TV panels
Wikipedia entries   Facebook or Twitter accounts

Think of the lowly city mouse   and how we treat each other
Our own children   Those who are old and alone

The Death of a Thousand Cuts

No one blow alone is lethal   The poison builds slowly
healing seductive promising release   only to be opened
at another time   another place *Lingchi*   the death
of a thousand cuts   Torture reserved for the vilest of deeds
or for the rebel   the one who doesn't fit   The ultimate warning
where not to entrust the heart   *Lingchi*   in modern parlance
creeping normality   unacceptable propositions occurring
in small unnoticeable increments until damage is irrevocable
Ice melting into water   dissolving from below
filling the vastness of an ocean   As islands are
swallowed up   populations displaced *Live somewhere else
leave what you love   move on*   As if love were a subway stop
as if you were holding up a restless queue
when what is dear to you is sliced away   First a finger
then an arm   a leg   the heart *Lingchi*   the scar remains
a network of twisted veins   The soul bleeds red
How long before the point of no return is reached

Reminiscences

For Cuba & for Meg

1.
Speaking to you   I was reminded
of those weeks   how far they seem
distant & yet   how strong

speaking to you

words fail me now   often
I sit for hours   without speech
images stray through my mind   songs

as I work a feeling of hunger   and then
of pain

Sometimes   no often   it is harder to remember   and then
on the faces   I discover it   in the streets as I walk
learning to look out boldly   into those eyes

it is not despair that turns them away   but hope
you asked why & that is the answer

refusing solace   refusing their dark places
their tombs

I sicken of those eyes   their sharp edges   their
wit   I sicken of the sophistication
of those eyes

    by their death   they remind me

    as those others did

                that winter

    so few weeks ago (we spoke together then)

    as they did

        by their life

2.

It is the song that has meaning   I heard them
sing   We heard them   in their winter   Their
hands   their voices   the song   as the poem
its words strong

& behind the words   the meaning   the syllables
the depth

There is this pain inside me   For years now
 I have known it   This pain   This companion of
mine

It reduces things cleverly this friend

What is greater than I

                              it croons to me
it sings to me

          What is greater than I

There are things greater   good   good   good

good   What are they

What is more important than this pain

How cleverly it reduces things   this ache
in my side

& those weeks made it deeper   I know now

what caused it   & that it will never leave

3.
It reminded me   your voice   of those days
The sea outside my window   I could never live long
beyond the reach of sea   At least sensing it there
around me   its song   even its silence   Always
I have lived near water   & there   it surrounded me

The East River is not an ocean
Is not beautiful like that sea
Does not break against the streets
furious   & then   calm

But it is water   & every now and then a boat passes
& the stillness of it   even the darkness
sometimes

& I see into it as one looks into water

with the backs of the eye

4.
It is not finished   is never over
Repeating again and again   Each time holding
the balance   tipping it
forward

        The revolution is for people
        they said   but it was not
        their words

                        it was them

        the way they were   the way they spoke

It was as hard to carry as water

And now months later   I have begun to
live   to speak   the change

the words written in blood in pain

You could scream it in the streets
and who would listen

But the scream remains   the sound of it
like the sound of your voice   and those
others   like their memory   like water

changing   as it flows

Morning Poem

There's always plenty of time
until it runs out on us
But you can't rush things either
They grow at their own speed
reaching for a point of contact
of their own

I am plagued with impatience
inertia
          the two extremes
the edges of everything
Those two things also
being one

Some people build homes   houses
of themselves   I think of Jung
his circular walls
                    years of
thought enclosing his body
Trapped in his own ideas

Others travel the streets
planting themselves in their
sidewalks
          Their bodies a motion
more like a dance

And some try both worlds
multiple existences

                     are makers of life
Patience is part of it   but more
To have a vision   To make it
real

      Can you see what I'm saying
How time itself is our enemy
our friend   How we trap ourselves
in vision

          But how it also opens

                        out

can lead us forward
How we lose things only to find
them again

         Only to find ourselves
different   at the same place

Listen   this morning the world closes
and opens at my fingertips   The sun
is bright   draws me to it
But I sit in a room cluttered with
memories books old pieces of furniture
old pieces of myself

I am inside
         and outside
of it all
I reach out
with what is behind me
I live my death
         am captured
in my life

Long Division

Nothing ever really seems to add up
My mother aged   frail   at seventy-eight
But I don't feel old   Don't feel any different
than I ever did

No different than fifty long years past
before her marriage drained sustained her
with rings and furs   a crazed husband's
unloaded gun pressed against her willing throat

Another piece of meaningless melodrama
in a world where children starve   old people die
lacking a few dollars to pay their bills

She used her talent looks to marry money
tossed her only daughter aside   a complication
An imagined contender for her throne

I could have loved you forever Mom   if you had let me
As it was I left   gave you hardly a backward glance
kept you from becoming my world

only to find the world becoming you

It's not my childhood that betrays me
I've digested that   spit out what I couldn't use
It's a world that's taken on your face
the duplicity of your tongue   your style

Alone at night sensation sinks too deep
In the mind's open cavern language
disappears   Everything is washed away

Even knowing what is real   How righteous anger
saves   Whether I will it or no
Her voice remains

Separation

Muffled by windows closed
against early spring chill   street noise
merges into a monotonous hum
The discordant drumbeat of car radios
as they whip by   A lone drunk
screaming his complaints to empty
sidewalks   The usual detritus
of late Manhattan nights

Sitting inside   eyes half closed
everything blurs into equal focus
The ever-present pile of books lining
shelves tables floor   A glass mug
A pack of gum   A shiny metal letter
opener   A statue of Guanyin
Bodhisattva of mercy   compassion

I see no separation between
these familiar objects   Nothing
stands out is featured in the foreground
Everything focused in equilibrium
perfectly attuned

How different from the night
another lifetime past   two small pills
opening a world through the pupil
of my eye   purple   brilliant
terrifying   as it confronted me
as I gazed into it   as I walked
into it   driven by anger   despair

pushing myself relentlessly
into its depths   the room swirling in
undulating waves of light
Everything around me dissolving
discarded   rejected   until finally
grasping the absurdity of the scene
my part in it   humor prevailed

This evening as I sit at my desk
grounded in present awareness
my cellphone rings abruptly
Attention snaps back shifting objects
once more into perspective

Unity elusive persists   a background hum
as insubstantial as the muffled figures
outside   in the night

The Tears of Things

Will they cry for us when we have gone
the objects that adorn our lives
When we have left   will they miss our touch
our need for them

Do they know they are the chosen ones
or do they fear we will tire of them
set them aside   bound as they are by our desire
not theirs

A ball point pen   white   with gold bands
imported from France   birthday gift
from a beloved friend   A fountain pen
sun yellow   with black enamel tip
Relics of an earlier age

Forty Oz books hidden from prying eyes
Well-worn novels   books of religion
philosophy the occult   long out of print
All those books we hold dear   have kept through years
with leather bindings   colorful illustrations
childhood dreams

The magazines we treasure   worthless to others
A college t-shirt   now sizes too small
A pair of boots   useless   but prized
A turquoise necklace from an old lover
too full of memories to wear

All the things we refuse to throw away
Each one holding a piece of our past

No longer here   people may cry for us
but even those who hold us dear
at a certain point move on   Our objects
belong to us alone   We have left part of ourselves
behind in them

Lacrimae rerum: the tears of things
Do they love us as we love them
Will they weep for us when we have gone

Autumn Song

I would like to believe it is summer
that years have brought me to a ripening
fruit bursting forth from branches
heavy with sweet juices   still steadfast
on green and tender limbs

But yesterday I saw one leaf fade   and then another
the green turning to red to brown to yellow
Burnt ragged by decades of heat
and sun I felt winter stalking my roots
starting as it does below the surface
deep beneath the ground

I fear the coming showers of color
violet magenta orange draping themselves around me
clothing me in lost moments   expectations passed
I search desperately for ways to clear the debris
free myself   but time betrays me
Snow draws near

From the Child Who Finally Understands

Grandmother's prized possession
the feather mattress she carried on her back
across a continent   seemed light to her
she claimed in later years

So said my mother   The only detail of her mother
she ever shared   As if she were surprised herself
an object so mundane could carry
such importance

Only one of her many burdens
perhaps grandmother believed the feathers
nesting on her shoulders could take wing
and ease her   on her way

Some children knew the paths she traveled
journeyed with her   shared the weight
Some were too young Others raised in a country
foreign to her birth

As for me   I realize now what I can never know
can never understand   except in the legacy
my parents marked me with   that carries down
from generation to generation   rooted
in our blood

There Is Something Called Longing

so fragile   it must never be spoken
The wind leaves its mark with invisible palms
The face of the wind is silence
But all this is a facade for something
so simple it defies definition
The world is terrible   huge   beyond
our control   As babies we knew it
As adults we had to pretend
to forget   Longing is part of remembering
and so we declare independence
think we have got it beat   think it
no longer matters
Yet we must fight the distance
with what sustenance   but each other

Cantos for Elegua

1.
Elegua is the guardian of the crossroads
Elegua changes your life Elegua protects
passageways what enters and leaves Elegua
has a knife on his head It cuts through deception
Scoundrels beware! Elegua is a trickster
His colors are red and black The colors of anarchy
revolution

Summon Elegua first with drums and dance and song
It is Elegua who bridges the human and the divine
The Highest without form or words speaks through Elegua
Elegua translates many languages Elegua is a go-between
Elegua is the mouth that devours His appetite is insatiable
Elegua gives back what he takes He is generous to a fault

Elegua has the-power-to-make-things-happen
Elegua spins us like a top Which direction shall we take?
Elegua guides us down paths we would never choose
Elegua teaches us without him we would be lost
Power lies on the other side of habit Elegua breaks routine
Elegua kicks you out of bed with one swift kick

Elegua smiles Elegua has seashells for eyes and mouth
Elegua tucks you in at night Elegua demands respect
Honor Elegua with caramels and rum
Burn a red candle in his name

2.

Elegua translates words of power   knowing full well
those who carry language bear the brunt
of what they speak The burden of meaning
is thrust upon them Should I then refuse words
embrace instead sweet Asphodel like
Williams or the darker nightmare vision

of Baudelaire   his flowers of sin
and shame   or should I start with the way
your hand felt as it carelessly brushed mine
How I wanted to hold it   tight   against me
Nothing is as simple as it seems The way letters flow

one into the other their shape what they signify
A street lamp thick with soot Icicles on a branch
heavy with the weight of water frozen to its
spine All these are words like any other

In the beginning the word was spoken
into the void And from that sound came life
Mortals even gods can turn their backs on meaning
voice senseless phrases nonsense syllables
pass them off for speech

but Elegua is not fooled All ceremonies begin
and end with him

Lilith of the Wildwood, of the Fair Places

And Lilith left Adam and went to seek her own place
and the gates were closed behind her and her name
was stricken from the Book of Life

1.
And how does one begin again

(Each time, each poem, each line, word, syllable
Each motion of the arms, the legs
a new beginning)

women   women surround me
images of women   their faces
I   who for years   pretended them away
pretended away their names   their faces
myself   what I am   pretended it away

as a name exists to confine to define confine
define   woman   the name   the word   the definition
the meaning beyond the word   the prism   prison
beyond the word

to pretend it away

2.
It's the things we feel most
we never say   for fear perhaps
that by saying them   the things we care most
for   will vanish
                    Love is most like that
is the unsaid thing   behind the things we do
when we care most

3.
to be an outcast   an outlaw
to stand apart from the law   the words
of the law
                    outlaw
                        outcast

cast out   cast out by her own will
refusing anything but her own place
a place apart from any other
                        her own

I do not have to read her legend in the ancient book
I do not have to read their lies
She is here   inside me
I reach to touch her

my body my breath my life

4.

To fear you	is to fear myself
To hate you	is to hate myself
To desire you	is to desire myself
To love you	is to love myself

Lilith of the Wildwood
Lilith of the Fair Places

who eats her own children
who is cursed of god

Mother of us all

Incantation

Of course how could it be any different
our first encounter   what goes in the mouth
what comes out in the way of words
or love   No day is new   we carry years into each dawn
Where is the detail in all this   who bears its name
We are human beings   a people who herd
Burdened with imagination wonder
we keen into the night   The joke's on us
played out by the greatest trickster of them all
An open mouth can never be filled   Emptiness is pure
desire   The language of the gods is food

Sanctuary

There are some people
who will never be safe
moving from country to country
over generations

There are some people
who will never feel safe
taught by fearful parents to
keep "the other" at arm's length

A rabbi declares his suitcase packed
ready to go   He has dual citizenship
not with Israel   with a Germany
repentant of unspeakable slaughter
An irony of history

You can retreat to your room
pull up the walls like a second skin
become invisible   silent
but you are still not safe

No walls are thick enough
No skin is thick enough

Despite impassioned rhetoric
facile slogans fantasy solutions
only one thing is certain
If the oppressed becomes oppressor
the cycle repeats

It Was Easier Then

Everything always seems easier in retrospect
when the stakes were lower
the odds   evened out by time

It was easier decades ago
the sixties   seventies
Easier when we lost the war
(no one likes to be a loser)
Easier to have heroes you could support
Ho Chi Minh Haydée Santamaría
George Jackson Fred Hampton
Rosa Parks Lolita Lebron Assata Shakur
Martin Luther King Malcolm X

It was easier to be twenty
the future interminable
the past a history lesson   words on a page
written in script   not blood
not your own   not yet

It was easier at thirty   at forty
It was easier last year
yesterday   ten minutes ago
one second before now

Then is always easier
than *now*

For those who dare look up   out of themselves
past their own eyebrows   the ridges of their nose
the corners of their shoes   they know
the struggle continues   outlasts us all

Today is after all only the continuation of then
Tomorrow   the extension of today

Whoever said the journey had an end
Whoever set a time   proscribed a date

Reflection

I remember the ocean   calm
in the morning   Its waves slowly
beating   white   against the shore
The stillness of the morning
A patina reflected on the ocean's skin
defying the relentlessness of weather
Life struggling to survive its depths

It seems so long ago I sat
at the water's edge   memory receding
then churning forward slowly
as the tide   The evening I met you
The sun beginning to set   The dense outline
 of your form   The way your shadow played
against the light

Night light in the city also comes in waves
Ruled by traffic signals   cars stop and start
street lamps outline the passage
of hurrying feet   Some poems are city nights
blazing with noise drumbeat shouts of the young
loud   boisterous   echoing off buildings
daring all to hear

Some poems are like this one   like age
placid in tone   ocean rhythms hidden
a pulse faintly beating   body still
lips pursed Words nesting quietly
against the heart

Spring

Before flowers came
the earth was dust and rock
Reptiles trod slowly on a land
where giants roamed   until one day
the wind   relentless   without mercy

carried a first seed in its fist
and then another   and another
until our world was populated
with richer hues   flowers and insects
A place where humans could survive

As millions of years ago
flowers transformed the earth
so today do we   Our blossoms
of differing hues patterns   alive
in flesh   and dream

Generations carried by
wind pushing   against dirt
and stone   Flowers germinating
inside us   waiting for us
to bring them into light

LGBTQIA+ PRIDE 2021
with kudos to Loren Isley

The Dreams That Haunt Me

Asleep   dreams slide away
careen down dark tunnels
into day   The exam unstudied for
The poetry reading with poems
left behind   Lost on the subway
in Brooklyn   or the Bronx
trying to get home

Awake   everything speeds past me
The present   instantaneous
like lightning on a summer evening
punctuated by the insatiable appetite
of rain

A Poem That Starts in Winter

This is a poem for people without a history
whatever their color   whatever their race
who can't remember their mother ever holding them
talking to them about their past
Who find themselves in unknown places
without instructions & without a guide

This is a poem for the children of immigrants
whose parents wanted so much to forget to leave behind
the places they were born   the places they fled
they never spoke of those days to their children
never even told them their grandparents' names
Who died leaving their children lost   and restless
rootless   hungry

This is a poem that starts in winter
but never ends   A poem about people
about individuals   with specific features
Proper names

This is a poem for Sarah whose mother was Jewish
but no one could tell   She had blond hair blue eyes
It was 1939   She taught Sarah a lesson about vision
how to make people see past you   how to hide
In moments of doubt they would always throw it in your face
You could count on it
"Dirty Jew"

This is a poem about words

This is a poem about Sarah's mother
Who never stepped inside a synagogue after the age of eight
Who never forgave her own parents for what she was born
an immigrant   poor
Who lived her contradictions until the day she died
Who left her lie behind her   A legacy drawn
in her daughter's face

This is a poem for Sarah's mother   A poem about words

This is a poem for Barbara   1961   Whose father warned her
if she were involved with those radicals at Berkeley those "Reds"
he would be the first to give her name to the FBI   to turn her in
She never doubted he was serious   She learned that day never
to trust   & never to speak

This is a poem about trust

This is a poem for Carole who cried out in shame
discovering her ancestors had killed & robbed
To gain a country   Carole who had a history
She no longer wished to claim

This is a poem for a Vietnamese poet   Havana, 1969
who praised three young Americans for their courage
standing against their own country   their own people
for what they felt right   He had no choice
was forced to fight   No virtue in that
They thought him too generous   mistaken at best
But still it helped   But still it healed

It was winter then too

This is a poem about digging images from rage
when all else fails   when there is no common past
An anger imbedded so deeply
it survives

This is a poem about war

This is a poem for Brenda   who fell in love with a woman
years before it became a political act
Who decades later still stumbles over words long forbidden
jealous of those who proclaim their love nonchalantly
"Lesbian"

This is a poem for Brenda
This is a poem about words
A poem about winter   A poem about war

This is a poem for those caught between worlds
squeezed between times   for people without a history
who connect with no ancestral past

This is a poem about them   about me

This is a poem about words like dialogue compassion
which have yet to appear   but people this poem
About war contradiction rage choice anger
trust

This is a poem that starts in winter
but never ends

This is a poem about people   individuals
with specific features
Proper names

Migration

Birds fly south   chained to the wind   They are wild
not free   There is a difference   They move
without reflection   choice   driven by instincts
they cannot begin to understand
What use are words against such need
I thought I could lose my self in wings
but I am held by memory desire
imagined futures Citizens of air of water
earth and sea   we are sisters and brothers
bound together by a destination that calls us
in our blood But only I can turn around
fly north   change direction return again
fly south into the wind

First Snow

Frozen into unchanging patterns
snow crystals drift to earth   first gentle
then violent   blown by fierce gusts of wind
no two alike   an infinity of difference

The flakes   ephemeral   dissolve as they fall
strike the pavement   merge together
pause for an instant   then suddenly are gone

In the morning clouds disperse   The sun brilliant
turns snow into mirror   a glazed surface
reflecting back into the seemingly endless blue
of sky

It's times like these   I most miss your warmth
another's eyes to share the winter's light
when memory cannot suffice   and even dreams
that come so seldom   are so easily forgotten

Searching further and further backward
into space   shattering atoms into fragments
we theorize a multiverse of choices   directions
worlds upon worlds

longing for something that might never
be found   was right in front of us
all along

Love Poem

if I could hold you
if I could wake up in the morning
and see your face
if I could touch you
if I could see you as you go to sleep
if I could feel you close
beside me   if I could reach out to you
touch you   in my need

time drifts endlessly   like water
like this afternoon
the breeze as it drifts
through my window
surrounds me   as thoughts of you
as breath of you
as I see you
as I wait for you
the inevitability of you
as I am surrounded by you
by my love of you
as I waken into life

my words   in silence
my love   in silence
the quiet of the afternoon
the curve of your face
your features   the way
you talk   the way you drift
in my thoughts endlessly
like time

if you were to ask me what defines me
how I place myself in this world
I would say this poem
is the center of it   is the core
that I reach toward the world
as I reach toward you
as one who wants to reach out
endlessly   who wants to open out
endlessly   who wants to feel
endlessly   that question
that is our lives

The Meeting

For Norma, New York, 1962

1.
To touch your face
To touch your arms
To touch your waist
To touch your thighs

To touch your sex

To hold it soft against my check
To breathe it slow against my lips
To hold you close against my breast

My love

2.
Old as the woman moaning songs
from her chill staccato walls
Old as that The touch between us
The chant filtering through coarse
night sounds The touch between us

Can I name you The words that lie against
me Soft against the night Can I call you
The night itself close upon my thighs

To hold you near
To touch your lips
To hold you close as my own breath

3.

Touched so deeply that tears come
unnoticed And without pain That once
were central And only pain

It is here between us Not ourselves
But what is here In this space

Touched so deeply that love comes
unnoticed And without pain That once
was central And only pain

4.

Rain glides in two dimensions The window
holding it to my face As I hold you As I
place my knuckles to your forehead Moving from
my touch

The vision two dimensions The surface
rigid As we reach toward it To find it
different But still there cool under our touch

5.

I would hold you gently
Throw myself against you as
the rain   Talk to you of
small things   As you would
touch a child   Or yourself
small and vulnerable to even
the slightest breath

6.

No longer afraid   The touch of you deeper
than any fear   Deeper than your naked form
The single syllable of your name

As I touch your body
As I touch the earth
As I touch this paper
As I touch each word

It is everywhere   This night and the
outline of our form   As we are together
Without boundary   Without dimension

As I touch the depth of you   My love

The Philosopher's Stone

What is the art that binds darkness and light
female and male   all oppositions
transcends dichotomies in that creative impulse

that gathers together out of the limitations
of time   what was lost in the first act
of creation by division

when zero became one   became two
then three   A multiplicity of words and
hearts   exemplified in a Forbidden Tree

A woman clothed in green
her garment adorned with spiders
flowers   stirs water into a vessel where

animals drink   their bodies parched
starved   their feet suspended over beds
of fire   All things divided unite in her hands

as water turns into blood   blood into
water   in the sacred chalice that feeds
the lion and the eagle at her feet

The alchemical stone remains invisible
but like the wind   moves everything in its path
as blood calls to blood   life to life

                              after XIV Trumps: The Thoth Tarot

The Final Cause

1.
Bound to the actual   What then can one make
of that which draws one near   Each thing tends
toward its own completion   What I am
What hurts me when it leaves

Memory takes place in an instant   This world
This formation of the lips   I cannot help
remembering

I want to be alone with my love
I want to be alone with that one voice
I want to be alone with the extremity of my love

With what delicacy   With what desire
does an arm of grass await
the rain

2.
How many times have I heard your voice
I am lifted by its seasons You hold my form
in your words It moves without my knowledge
to a place which I can only later know

I am dizzy with fear
Space has no conscience
I am without mystery
You center my darkness in your soil
The rain has no companion
but my years

3.
There is more than this one dream
You lie before me vast incomprehensible
I release myself into your arms

Joy holds me Terror holds me
I become part of what it is
to be

     All knowledge is re-
     turning All love
     becomes as one I
     trust what listens

The dream descends There is nothing here
but the sky laughter of a child Would you
consider her excuses as a prayer

4.

White smoke in your hands
The willow withers   Sound lacks
conclusion Your voice harbors
my distance I search the moon
Light falls on my cheek

I lie without weapons I await your desire
Only do not order me too soon
into the night   My heart remains burdened
with the sun

5.

There is no simple path Only thought
is without distraction Fire edges
the morning Pigeons nest on the surfaces
of my eyes Wind colors my ankles
They do not believe in silence
This thing that is That must remain
my own

The Palace of the Lowest Moon

1.
The animal crawls   sexless   blind   part of the organism of
the queen   Driven as a cell   in its journey of bone and
blood

>   They march in rows   Their moments instinctive
>   as growth itself   The red ant   Its face turned
>   toward the earth

The ant hill follows its weaving pattern   Its skin
As it builds itself   frame by frame   on skeletons
of wind and dirt

>   Tell me of silence
>   Of your touch   The
>   one moment   For that
>   moment is love   When
>   the body bends back-
>   ward away from the
>   sharp hard bite of
>   flesh

The ant hill resembles the tension of your leg   As it
covers me   Turning me toward   and away from   light

You tell me it is better to know   To count the cells on their
passage across the blood   Yes   And I close my eyes   Rest my
arms on the cold hard table   finding in its pain   A kind
of rest

2.

The queen breathes   Her soldiers flock around the borders
of her palace   Even light cannot disturb her in her task
To bring her muscles   flowing   into life

Why do they move   Why

The skin of the queen   gray   needing no color
Her purpose to be purpose   Her knowledge
the flesh of the palace

And the blood of our own arms is the answer

How many years they move   Carrying life into
that body   We hold this many lives in our one
outline   This many lives hold us in their
blood

     As we spin here   Caught above the
     center of the earth   While far
     beneath us other structures sway
     and breathe

3.
I came before you with a whine
Afraid of the sound of my own
words

> The queen waits   unaware   knowing
> somewhere an order exists that is
> her life

I told you not to speak
In your voice was too much
truth   Fear is the end of
the search
            And knowing
so much death   Is that
also a part of it

> Dark   Dark   The night   Dark
> The entrance to the palace
> *I came before you with a whine*
> *Afraid of the sound of my own*
> *words*

How long can one wait   The clatter of the
ants breathing into my lips   The ants
Their bodies folding deep into the soft
arms of the earth

4.

Finally the snow   Covering bare grounds with
thin white ash   Forcing animals down   Down into
the damp recesses of the earth

And still long after it stands
Impervious to the gentle whimpering
of the rain

> Holding you   Your body secure
> White layers of snow cutting
> deep   into my eyes

I would separate myself   Hold this sight from my
arms   To walk into the snow   Dying only as part
of the motion

> Caught in this impossible act
> Order no more than our own
> perception

5.

Let what is dead   die   Firm walls around the
cavern green with time   Feeling translated into
words

> Where is your hand   Your
> promise no longer where
> there is no land   no wa-
> ter   Oceans beating over
> rock and you so far   Your
> words like rock and parched
> like sand

It cannot happen   Until speech itself is
mute   We are not centers in that sense
The mindless ant carrying worlds upon its
tendrils

> I live in the palace of
> the lowest moon   I
> reach the ocean in my
> garden   The fish that
> dance upon my table spin
> the riddles of my name
> Your face is with me
> as my own

Demetria Martínez:

Thank you to poet John Roche at Jules' Poetry Playhouse for dreaming up the title for my writing retreats, Poetry in Dangerous Times, which became the title of this book.

This work would not exist if not for the love, support, and encouragement of my wife, Camilla Bustamante: You have been with me on this journey in the dark and in the light. I'm so very grateful.

Thanks also to my family, especially Dad, Ted Martínez. Our daily phone calls, and your reminders—*I'm proud of you, mijita*—have sweetened my days.

To Mary Paltrow, thank you for teaching me that our issues are in our tissues, and that we must move, move, move—and breathe.

And finally, thank you to Jeffrey Katzman, MD. Together we have built a house for my grief, a house for my joy. And the house stands.

Some of my poems in this collection have been previously published. The poems "Birthday," "La Promesa," "Rear Views," and "Clock" were first published in *The*

Devil's Workshop (University of Arizona Press, 2002). The poems "Wanted," "The Dress Daisy Gave Me," and "You Tell Me There Is a Place" (as "Untitled #1") were first published in *Breathing Between the Lines* (University of Oklahoma Press, 1997). The poem "Nativity: For Two Salvadoran Women" first appeared in *Three Times A Woman* (Bilingual Review Press, 1989). The poems "Death" and "Advent" appeared in the Uruguayan literary review *ISTA* #4 (2024).

Susan Sherman:

My gratitude to my dear friend Margaret Randall for her encouragement and support for more than sixty years. To compañeras Colleen McKay, who has contributed so much to my work and to my life, and Laraine Goodman for her invaluable friendship. To those alternative presses that have made my work available, including a triple thanks for his dedication and tender care collaborating on this project to Casa Urraca Press editor and publisher Zach Hively. And finally to editor and publisher Julie R. Enszer for featuring *IKON* magazine in Sinister Wisdom #136 and for making the complete archive of Series Two available online at the Lesbian Poetry Archive.

Some of the work contained in the present volume has appeared in my previous books, including *With Anger/ With Love: Selections: Poems & Prose 1963–1972* (Mulch Press, 1974), *We Stand Our Ground: Three Women, Their Vision, Their Poems* (IKON Press, 1988), *The Color of the Heart: Writing from Struggle & Change 1959–1990* (Curbstone, 1990), and *The Light That Puts an End to Dreams* (Wings Press, 2012).

Some of the work published here has appeared in the following magazines and anthologies: *13th Moon*; *Art Against Apartheid: Works for Freedom*; *Bridges*; *The Café Review*; *Changer L'Amérique: Anthologie de la Poésie Protestataire des USA (1980–1995)*; *Conditions*;

Downtown Poets; *An Ear to the Ground*; *El Corno Emplumado*; *A Gathering of the Tribes*; *Heresies*; *IKON*; *Learning Our Way*; *Lesbian Culture: An Anthology*; *LibeRATion Newspaper*; *Long Shot*; *The Malpais Review*; *The Nation*; *Poetry*; *Poetry Like Bread*; *Sinister Wisdom*; and *Women Brave in the Face of Danger*.

Demetria Martínez, writer, poet, and activist, was born and raised in Albuquerque. She earned a BA from the Woodrow Wilson School of Public and International Affairs from Princeton University. As a journalist, she covered religion for the *Albuquerque Journal* and was a national news editor and a columnist for the *National Catholic Reporter*.

Martínez's widely translated novel *Mother Tongue* (Ballantine), set during the Sanctuary Movement, won a Western States Book Award. The novel was inspired by her 1987 indictment on charges of conspiracy in connection with allegedly transporting Central American refugees into the United States. The U.S. government attempted to use her poem "Nativity: For Two Salvadoran Women, 1986–1987" against her. A jury acquitted her on First Amendment grounds. Martínez went on to speak about this book in El Salvador, at a conference on post-war Salvadoran literature. Alice Walker called *Mother Tongue* "a great beauty of a book" and said, "I am so proud of Demetria Martínez for standing with and for the disappeared."

Martínez's poetry collections include *The Devil's Workshop* (University of Arizona Press), *Breathing Between the Lines* (University of Oklahoma Press), and *Turning*, which appeared in an anthology of three Chicana poets, *Three Times A Woman* (Bilingual Review Press). She is the author of a short story collection, *The Block Captain's Daughter*, which received the 2013 American Book Award from the Before Columbus Foundation. Martínez coauthored *These People Want to Work: Immigration Reform* with former Oklahoma Senator Fred Harris. Her essay collection, *Confessions of a Berlitz-Tape Chicana* (University of Oklahoma Press), won an International Latino Book Award. She has also received the Luis Leal Award for Distinction in Chicano/Latino Literature. With Rosalee Montoya-Read, she coauthored *Grandpa's Magic Tortilla* (University of New Mexico Press), which won a New Mexico Book Award. In 2024, her translations of her grandfather's corridos—which she worked on with Mexican poet Hector Contreras and New Mexican folklorist Enrique Lamadrid—appeared in the *New Mexico Historical Review* along with an essay about his career.

Martínez lives with her wife in La Cienega, New Mexico.

Susan Sherman is a poet, playwright, essayist, and editor and co-founder of *IKON* magazine. She graduated from UC Berkeley in 1961 and moved to New York. In the sixties, she was a poetry editor for *The Nation* and a poetry editor and theater critic for *The Village Voice*. She joined the poetry circle at the Deux Megots coffee house, later running the open readings at the Metro Café with Allen Katzman and Carol Bergé. In 1968, she traveled to Cuba to attend the Cultural Congress of Havana and returned for an extended stay a year later to receive medical treatment. She received an MA in philosophy from Hunter College, taught at the Free School of New York and the Alternate U., edited the first series of *IKON* magazine, and opened IKONbooks, a bookstore which served as a cultural and movement center.

In 1970, she helped coordinate the Fifth Street Women's Building squatter's action, during which she became active in the feminist and the gay liberation movements. In the 1980s, she reintroduced *IKON* as a feminist magazine. In 2004, she participated in the successful struggle to unionize Parsons School of Design part-time faculty and remained an active member of ACT-UAW Local 7902 throughout the strike of 2022. She finally retired in 2023 after more than forty years of teaching.

Sherman has had twelve off-off-Broadway productions and published an adaptation of a Cuban play by Pepe Carril, *Shango de Ima* (Doubleday), which won 11 AUDELCO awards for a 1996 revival produced by the Nuyorican Poets Café. She published her memoir, *America's Child: A Woman's Journey Through the Radical Sixties* (Curbstone), in 2007 to critical acclaim. She has published seven collections of poetry. Her collection *The Light That Puts an End to Dreams* (Wings Press) was a finalist for the Publishing Triangle's Audre Lorde Award for Lesbian Poetry. She has also published a book of short fiction, *Nirvana on Ninth Street* (Wings Press), and a collaborative book of dialogue and poetry, *We Stand Our Ground*, with Kimiko Hahn and Gale P. Jackson (IKONbooks). Her correspondence with poet and activist Margaret Randall is featured in Randall's recent book *Letters from the Edge: Outrider Conversations* (New Village Press).

Her awards include the University Poetry Prize from UC Berkeley, a fellowship from the New York Foundation for the Arts for Creative Nonfiction Literature, a New York Foundation for the Arts fellowship for Poetry, a Puffin Foundation Grant, a Creative Artist's Public Service Grant for poetry, and editors' awards from the Coordinating Council of Literary Magazines and the New York State Council on the Arts.

For more information, visit susansherman.com.

Bookmania, the body typeface for this book, combines the sturdy elegance of the original Bookman Oldstyle with the swashy exuberance of the Bookmans of the 1960s. Unlike some Bookman revivals, it retains the original classic sloped roman for the italic. This typeface was designed by Mark Simonson, from Mark Simonson Studio.

Playfair, the header and title typeface for this book, is a transitional design. In the European Enlightenment in the late eighteenth century, broad nib quills were replaced by pointed steel pens as the popular writing tool of the day. It became fashionable to print letterforms of high contrast and delicate hairlines that were increasingly detached from the written letterforms. This design lends itself to this period, and while it is not a revival of any particular design, it takes influence from the designs of John Baskerville and from "Scotch Roman" designs. This typeface was designed by Claus Eggers Sørensen.

Casa Urraca Press publishes poetry, fiction, creative nonfiction, and other creative works, emphasizing those with strong connection to New Mexico and the U.S. Southwest. Our part of the world is rich in literary talent, and the rest of the world deserves to experience our perspectives. So we champion books that belong in the conversation—books with the power, compassion, and variety to bring very different people closer together.

We were founded in the high desert somewhere near Abiquiú, New Mexico. To read more from our authors, register for writing workshops, and browse all available editions of our independently published books, visit us at casaurracapress.com.